TEACHING CITIZENSHIP THROUGH TRADITIONAL TALES

AGES 5 TO 7

SUE ELLIS & DEIRDRE GROGAN

© 2003 Scholastic Ltd
Text © Sue Ellis & Deirdre Grogan 2003

Published by Scholastic Ltd,
Villiers House,
Clarendon Avenue,
Leamington Spa,
Warwickshire CV32 5PR

Printed by Bell & Bain Ltd, Glasgow

1 2 3 4 5 6 7 8 9 0   3 4 5 6 7 8 9 0 1 2

British Library Cataloguing-in-Publication Data
A catalogue record for this book is
available from the British Library.

ISBN 0-439-98449-1

Authors
Sue Ellis &
Deirdre Grogan

Editor
Dulcie Booth

Assistant Editor
Clare Gallaher

Designers
Heather Sanneh &
Catherine Mason

Illustrations
Woody

Cover illustration
Louise Gardner &
Mark Preston/Illustration

INTRODUCTION

Teaching citizenship – why use this resource?

Citizenship requires an understanding of the moral values that underpin actions. Right and wrong are often presented as simple choices. However, context clouds moral decisions and young children need to learn how to make balanced judgements based on a consideration of all relevant factors within the situation.

When teachers pose moral dilemmas, children often supply answers that they think the teacher wants to hear, rather than answers that reflect their true beliefs or opinions. Moral issues posed in a fun, make-believe context can liberate children, allowing them to debate issues and think about consequences of decisions in a more open-ended manner.

This resource allows children to:

■ engage in honest debate about key citizenship concepts such as fairness, the nature of right and wrong, and the need for a balance between rights and responsibilities

■ explore and understand the process of making moral judgements and decisions

■ explore and develop their own understandings of human nature, motivations and relationships

■ consider the value, power and uses of money

■ explore the different ways in which situations can be interpreted and how their own views are informed by their own experiences.

Young children like receiving post. The letter format is particularly effective for this purpose because it is short, direct, demands a reply and requires children to give their own opinion. Because children are not writing directly to the teacher, they are more likely to put down what they really think and feel, rather than what they imagine the teacher would like them to say.

Working within the Literacy Hour

The tasks and activities support work for the Literacy Hour by introducing and reinforcing the letter format as well as persuasive and explanatory writing. Over several letters, children will become familiar with the layout and different genres. They know what 'job' their letter has to do and teachers can gradually withdraw the amount of support they give, enabling children to become independent writers. Reading letters written by others can raise children's awareness of the need to be clear and concise, and reinforce how the layout of a letter and the structure within it helps the reader to understand. Teachers will find that the letter-writing tasks fit neatly into a Literacy Hour format, as part of a PSHE and citizenship lesson, or can be set as a homework task.

The traditional tales

The letters cover ten traditional tales, briefly summarised below. The majority are well known, some may be less familiar. However, all tales appear regularly in fairy tale anthologies and series such as the Ladybird *Well Loved Tales* series, or Jonathan Langley's popular fairy tale series published by Picture Lions.

Goldilocks & the Three Bears

Goldilocks breaks into the Three Bears' cottage. She tastes their porridge (eating all of Baby Bear's), she tries out their chairs (breaking Baby Bear's) and their beds (falling asleep on Baby Bear's). When the Bears return, they discover someone has been eating their porridge, sitting in their chairs and sleeping in their beds. They find Goldilocks asleep, she wakes up and runs off.

The Three Little Pigs

The Three Little Pigs each build a house; one of straw, one of wood and one of bricks. When the big bad Wolf arrives, he huffs and puffs and blows down first the straw house (and the Pig takes refuge in the wooden house) and then the wooden house (the Pigs take refuge in the brick house). The Wolf cannot blow the brick house so he tries to climb down the chimney, but falls into a pot of boiling water, placed there by the clever Three Pigs.

Cinderella

Cinderella is badly treated by her two Ugly Sisters. The Prince invites everyone to a ball. The Ugly Sisters go, leaving

Cinderella to clean the house. Cinderella's Fairy Godmother appears and grants her wish to go to the ball but she must leave by midnight. The Prince falls in love with Cinderella. As she rushes away, she loses her glass slipper. The Prince determines that whoever fits the slipper will become his wife. Much to the Ugly Sisters' annoyance, Cinderella fits the shoe, marries the Prince and lives happily ever after.

Snow White & the Seven Dwarves

When the magic mirrors says that Snow White is 'the fairest of them all', she is cast out into the wood by her wicked stepmother. She lives with the Seven Dwarves and survives her stepmother's attempts to kill her (tightening her corset and a poisoned hairgrip). Eventually, she succumbs to a poisoned apple. A prince sees Snow White in her glass coffin and falls in love. As the coffin is being moved, the apple falls from her mouth and she is restored to good health.

Jack & the Beanstalk

Jack and his mother are very poor. He is sent to sell Daisy their cow but instead swaps her for magic beans. In anger, Jack's mother throws them out of the window and overnight a beanstalk grows. When Jack climbs the beanstalk he finds a Giant's castle. On successive trips, he steals money, a hen that lays golden eggs and finally gets caught taking a singing harp. The Giant is killed when Jack's mother cuts down the beanstalk whilst he is still on it, in pursuit of Jack.

The Seven Little Kids

Mother Goat leaves the Seven Little Kids alone with strict instructions not to open the door to anyone. The Wolf tries to gain entry, eventually tricking the kids into believing that he is their mother by encasing his paw in white dough and

swallowing a cherrystone to make his voice appropriate. Only one kid survives (by hiding in the clock-case). On her return, Mother Goat finds the Wolf, cuts him open to release her children and fills him with stones. When the Wolf tries next to drink from a well, he topples over and drowns.

Little Red Riding Hood

Red Riding Hood must take a basket of goodies to her sick granny. She is waylaid by the Wolf, who runs ahead to Granny's house. There, he disguises himself as Granny, after locking her in a cupboard. Red Riding Hood is suspicious (asking *What big eyes/ears/teeth you have, Granny…*). The Wolf tries to eat her, but Red Riding Hood is saved by the woodcutter. Granny is rescued from the cupboard and everyone lives happily ever after.

The Elves & the Shoemaker

The Shoemaker's business is not going well. One night the Elves make the most beautiful pair of shoes from his final piece of leather. Each night, they make more shoes. The Shoemaker becomes famous. As a gift to say thank you, he and his wife make the Elves clothes and shoes. The Elves move on, leaving the Shoemaker and his wife rich and happy.

The Three Billy Goats Gruff

The Billy Goats try to cross the bridge to eat the lush green grass. Underneath the bridge lives the Troll. The Little and Middle-Sized Billy Goats cross the bridge by persuading the Troll that the Big Billy Goat will provide a more satisfying meal and are allowed to cross. The Big Billy Goat tosses the Troll high into the air and crosses safely to the other side. All three Billy Goats live happily and get fat eating the lush grass.

Hansel and Gretel

Their wicked stepmother and weak father try to leave
Hansel and Gretel in the forest. On the first occasion,
Hansel and Gretel leave a trail of stones and are able to find
their way back. On the second occasion they leave
breadcrumbs which the birds eat all up and they are lost.
The children wander until they find a gingerbread house
made of sweets. They are discovered eating the house by
the witch who lives in it. She locks Hansel in a cage to
fatten him up to eat and makes Gretel work for her. On the
day Hansel is to be eaten, Gretel pushes the witch into her
own baking oven and releases Hansel. On returning to their
father, they find the stepmother has left and all three live
happily ever after.

How to use these letters

Introducing the letter

A fun way to introduce the first letter to young children is
by reading the relevant fairy tale. As you put the book
away, allow the letter, which of course will be in an
appropriately decorated and addressed envelope, to fall
from between the pages of the book. Let the children see
the address on the front of the envelope and help them to
read the letter out loud.

   Alternatively, if you are sure that all children in the class
will know the relevant fairy tale, the letter can be
'discovered' by the children – on someone's chair, in the
library corner, in the fairy tale book or be delivered to the
class by the caretaker, the school secretary, the headteacher
or a child from another class. We found that it was often
helpful to remind children of the fairy tale in question, even

when it was a fairy tale that was well known to them. It is therefore a good idea to have ensured that it has been read or discussed at some point before (but not necessarily immediately before) the letter arrives. Varying the time allowed to lapse between hearing the fairy tale and receiving the letter and varying the ways in which the letter arrives in class, stops the letters from becoming routine and predictable.

Older children can be introduced to the letter idea in a number of ways. One teacher showed the children books structured around the idea of letters, for example *The Jolly Postman* by Janet and Allan Ahlberg (Puffin) and *Little Wolf's Book of Badness* by Ian Whybrow (HarperCollins). She suggested that the class make their own books of letters by replying to different fairy tale characters' problems.

Another teacher established a regular 'Problem Tuesday' in the classroom; each week a different problem arrived. The teacher made a display area in which she put up the problem letter, a selection of the children's answers and headline banners asking the fundamental questions. This display became her teaching focus for discussion.

In both classes, the teachers made sure that the problem letters arrived in a variety of unexpected ways, sometimes addressed to the class and sometimes to the teacher or to groups of children.

Leading the initial discussion

It is a good idea to let a child, or a couple of children, open the letter and read it out to the class. Ask *What does that mean, exactly?* to give the children an opportunity to define the problem in their own words.

During the class discussion, elicit as many viewpoints as possible to help the children explore the full range of reasons and explanations behind their initial suggested advice. To do this successfully, it is important to remain non-committal and non-judgemental. We found it helpful to prompt the children to identify how their initial viewpoints relate to those expressed by others in the class and to emphasise the need to think through the consequences of actions. It is, however, unhelpful at this stage to discuss the consequences in detail or to push children into making a final judgement. Use phrases such as:

- That's an interesting point of view.
- Can you explain your thinking/reasoning behind that?
- That is a different opinion from… because…
- So you would agree/disagree with… because…
- That is one viewpoint, what do other people think?
- So you think…

Helping the children write their replies

Once all opinions have been elicited and explored, get the children to write their own replies to the letters. Before the children write, emphasise the importance of:

■ Being honest: they must give the advice they believe will work best, taking into account the whole situation.

■ Being clear: they must give their advice and also explain their reasons. Explain that reasons are important to allow the fairy tale character to choose between conflicting advice.

Whilst they are writing, comment on how clearly they are expressing and explaining their advice.

The fairy tale letters provide children with many repeated opportunities to write in the format of a letter and to write an explanatory argument. They therefore provide an excellent opportunity to teach children to become independent writers by gradually withdrawing the amount of help given with the format and layout, structure, language or strategic decision-making. Initially, you may need to provide support in the form of writing frames, teacher-modelling or checklist reminders. After writing several letters, children should become more independent, faster and more fluent as they become more familiar with the format and genre, and you should plan to withdraw the amount of support.

The letters can also be used as stimulus for the writing table. Simply introduce the letter to the whole class and hold a brief discussion, if necessary. Then put the letter on the writing table along with a picture of the main character, some key words and questions which will support the children in writing their replies and a postbox (it can be a simple box covered with red paper or an 'in-tray' with an appropriate label). You may like to give the children a choice of letter-writing paper and pens and allow them to choose which to use to write their letters.

Concluding discussions

Once they have written their letters, give the children an opportunity to read and discuss each other's work. This is important in helping children reflect on their own and each other's points of view, and also in helping them to understand what makes a piece of writing clear, easy to follow and convincing.

Select letters with different advice or with different reasons for the same advice and pose some of the key questions. Ask the children what they think, and why. At this point it is appropriate to:
- push children to think about the consequences
- encourage them to imagine what would happen if ideas were extrapolated to the whole of society, and
- encourage them to think of examples and counter-examples from the real world.

Many moral ideas/debates need time to 'cook' before people change their view. It is therefore not important that children make a firm decision. It is, however, useful to display the letter and a selection of the children's replies that illustrate different positions and the key questions in an accessible form so that children can read and re-read them at their leisure. We found that both a regular display space on the wall and display in the form of a book/folder placed in the library corner worked well; and that an A4 ring-binder folder with the letter on the front and the answers in transparent punched pockets was a quick and effective display mechanism.

It can be interesting to return to the children's letters after a few weeks and ask them whether their views on the big issues remain the same.

Choosing the letters

The letters vary in the type of issues they raise. Some are more appropriate for younger children and others may be more suitable for an older Key Stage 1 class. Broadly, letters at the start of the book are suitable for younger children; those towards the end deal with more complex content

issues and can be used for older classes. Start with a letter you think your class would enjoy and which raises issues that are important for the children.

All the letters encourage children to:
■ recognise right and wrong, fair and unfair and develop a more sophisticated understanding of these key concepts
■ share their opinions about things that matter to them
■ recognise and deal with feelings in a positive way
■ take part in simple debates about relevant issues
■ consider the choices people can make, and their consequences
■ make decisions by considering the value of alternative courses of action.

The chart on pages 12–13 indicates the particular issues or dilemmas raised by each letter. Use the chart to select particular letters that raise the citizenship issues that they would like to debate. For example, if you wanted to focus on 'making friends', you would then turn to look at letters 2, 9, 12, 14, 15, 18, 25, 36, 40 and 46. Within these letters, those nearest the beginning of the book (that is, those with the lowest numbers) are likely to be the most straightforward. However, the letters span different stories, and it may be that you want to select letters which relate to a specific fairy tale – either because it is one recently studied by the class, or a fairy tale with which the children are very familiar.

CHART TO SHOW THE CITIZENSHIP ISSUES RAISED IN EACH LETTER

CITIZENSHIP ISSUE / LETTER	1	2	3	4	5	6	7	8	9	10	11	12	13	14	15	16	17	18	19	20	21	22	23	24	25
▽ Developing good relationships and respecting the differences between people																									
Bullying																				✓				✓	✓
Aggressive behaviour																				✓					✓
Making friends			✓											✓	✓		✓							✓	
Forgiveness; when, how and why			✓						✓		✓	✓	✓	✓	✓							✓			
Saying sorry/making amends			✓								✓	✓	✓									✓	✓		
Trust; recognising and assessing motivations; assessing the value of a promise																						✓			
Negotiating solutions	✓			✓					✓		✓		✓								✓			✓	
Recognising/understanding others' feelings/points of view			✓				✓			✓	✓	✓	✓								✓		✓		✓
People developing and changing; can they change, what prompts change, how to recognise change			✓								✓	✓		✓								✓			
Saying thank you – when and how					✓										✓										
Recognising and controlling emotions						✓													✓	✓					
▽ Developing confidence and responsibility and making the most of their abilities																									
Importance of stating opinion and reasons	✓								✓							✓				✓				✓	
Recognising personal qualities/looking beyond the skin-deep features																									
Taking responsibility for one's own actions	✓		✓										✓												
Power, value and limits of money															✓	✓			✓						
Recognising people who can help						✓	✓			✓								✓		✓	✓				
Importance of explaining/discussing fears/emotions					✓							✓						✓							
Dealing with peer pressure					✓	✓	✓											✓		✓					
Setting simple goals				✓							✓							✓							
Loneliness		✓							✓		✓							✓							
▽ Preparing to play an active role as citizens																									·
Moral/immoral ways of persuasion	✓						✓					✓													
Rules																✓	✓		✓						
Sharing things			✓		✓			✓			✓		✓			✓				✓	✓	✓	✓		
Needs of self/others such as older/younger people					✓		✓	✓							✓				✓			✓			
Respect for others' property and rights			✓													✓	✓			✓					
Balancing current and future needs										✓															
Do ends justify means?								✓																	
Rights and responsibilities									✓		✓				✓					✓					
Recognising right and wrong									✓					✓				✓							✓
▽ Developing a healthy, safer lifestyle																									
Healthy diet	✓																								
Keeping safe outside																	✓		✓				✓		
Keeping clean/hygiene				✓			✓	✓								✓									
Keeping safe in the home							✓	✓										✓							

CITIZENSHIP ISSUE	27	28	29	30	31	32	33	34	35	36	37	38	39	40	41	42	43	44	45	46	47	48	49	50
Bullying	✓																							✓
Aggressive behaviour	✓	✓		✓		✓								✓					✓	✓			✓	
Making friends											✓			✓	✓						✓			
Forgiveness; when, how and why		✓				✓				✓	✓								✓	✓	✓			✓
Saying sorry/making amends		✓	✓											✓	✓									✓
Trust; recognising and assessing motivations; assessing the value of a promise										✓								✓		✓				
Negotiating solutions	✓			✓		✓	✓									✓						✓		
Recognising/understanding others' feelings/points of view	✓	✓		✓	✓	✓	✓								✓							✓	✓	
People developing and changing; can they change, what prompts change, how to recognise change	✓	✓		✓						✓					✓					✓				
Saying thank you – when and how													✓											
Recognising and controlling emotions	✓	✓		✓		✓							✓		✓				✓					
Importance of stating opinion and reasons	✓	✓		✓		✓									✓	✓		✓						✓
Recognising personal qualities/looking beyond the skin-deep features										✓								✓						
Taking responsibility for one's own actions				✓		✓						✓	✓											✓
Power, value and limits of money					✓																✓			
Recognising people who can help	✓											✓				✓		✓						
Importance of explaining/discussing fears/emotions		✓						✓							✓			✓						✓
Dealing with peer pressure									✓						✓									
Setting simple goals															✓									
Loneliness																								
Moral/immoral ways of persuasion	✓			✓		✓								✓	✓									✓
Rules						✓			✓					✓	✓									
Sharing things		✓														✓								✓
Needs of self/others such as older/younger people						✓								✓		✓								
Respect for others' property and rights		✓						✓						✓										✓
Balancing current and future needs		✓													✓						✓			
Do ends justify means?					✓																			
Rights and responsibilities		✓		✓		✓	✓									✓						✓	✓	
Recognising right and wrong						✓	✓						✓				✓	✓						✓
Healthy diet																							✓	
Keeping safe outside																					✓			
Keeping clean/hygiene																						✓		
Keeping safe in the home																								

Goldilocks & the Three Bears

1

Some prompt questions/points to think about

These questions/prompts may be raised before writing the letters or afterwards in a discussion of the views expressed in the children's letters. Some may make good headings/questions on a display of the children's letters.

- Do you ever feel like Baby Bear?
- You need to look at it from his mother's point of view: why might Baby Bear's mother be giving him porridge?
- What else could he have for a healthy breakfast?
- How could he persuade his mother to buy something else for breakfast?

- Are there some methods of persuasion that *shouldn't* be used? Why?
- What are the most successful ways to persuade people?
- Do parents have a right to tell children what to eat?

Bear Cottage

Wood Lane

Darksville

Monday

Dear Class

My mum keeps making me porridge for breakfast. I HATE porridge. What else can I eat, and how can I make her buy it?

Baby Bear

The Three Little Pigs

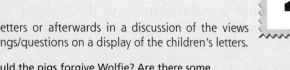

2

Some prompt questions/points to think about

These questions/prompts may be raised before writing the letters or afterwards in a discussion of the views expressed in the children's letters. Some may make good headings/questions on a display of the children's letters.

■ Do you think Wolfie is really sorry?
■ How can you show people you are sorry? How can you tell that someone is really sorry?
■ Can you *make* someone like you?
■ Can people who have done bad things change or will they always be bad?

■ Should the pigs forgive Wolfie? Are there some things that can never be forgiven?
■ Can you see this from the pigs' viewpoint/ Wolfie's viewpoint?

5 Windy Block
Stoney Hill

Thursday

Dear Class

Last year I blew down two of the Little Pigs' houses. I keep telling them I'm sorry, but they won't listen. How can I make them like me?

Wolfie

Cinderella

3

Some prompt questions/points to think about

These questions/prompts may be raised before writing the letters or afterwards in a discussion of the views expressed in the children's letters. Some may make good headings/questions on a display of the children's letters.

■ Can you think of someone you know that the Fairy Godmother might be able to help?

■ Can you think of people in the community/the wider world who might need help?

■ What are the different types of help people may require – material needs, emotional/social needs? (For example, companionship, confidence.)

■ What is the difference between needs and wants?

■ How could the Fairy Godmother weigh the different claims and decide whom to help? (What criteria should she use?)

■ Do all the things the children suggest actually need magic, or are some within our own/other people's control?

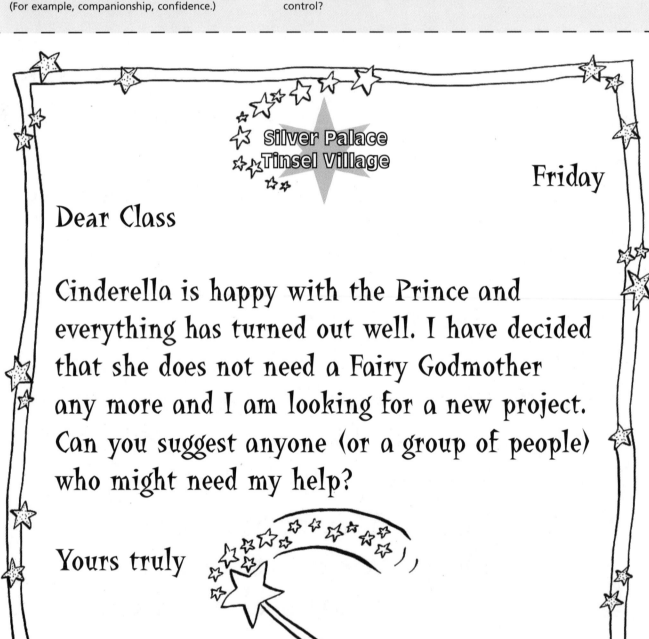

Silver Palace
Tinsel Village

Friday

Dear Class

Cinderella is happy with the Prince and everything has turned out well. I have decided that she does not need a Fairy Godmother any more and I am looking for a new project. Can you suggest anyone (or a group of people) who might need my help?

Yours truly

The Fairy Godmother

Snow White & the Seven Dwarves

4

Some prompt questions/points to think about

These questions/prompts may be raised before writing the letters or afterwards in a discussion of the views expressed in the children's letters. Some may make good headings/questions on a display of the children's letters.

■ Would it be a bad thing if no one did any cleaning?

■ Can a house (or person) be too clean? Too dirty? Why?

■ Are some cleaning jobs worse than others? Why?

■ Should everyone have to clean? Are there any acceptable reasons for opting out?

■ How can the Dwarves come to an agreement? What would you suggest if they can't agree?

■ Are some ways of resolving disagreements more/less productive than others?

■ How can the Dwarves remember who is to do what and when?

Little Cottage
Smallville

Wednesday

Dear Class

Since Snow White left we have been trying to keep our house clean and make sure we keep ourselves neat and tidy. We can't decide how many times a week we should wash the dishes, wash the windows and wash ourselves. Please help.

Yours

Doc   Grumpy   Sneezey

Bashful   Dopey   Happy   Sleepy

The Seven Dwarves

Jack & the Beanstalk

5

Some prompt questions/points to think about

These questions/prompts may be raised before writing the letters or afterwards in a discussion of the views expressed in the children's letters. Some may make good headings/questions on a display of the children's letters.

■ Is it necessary/important to say thank you, even if you will never see the person again? Why?

■ What are the different ways of saying thank you? (For example, sending a letter/card, doing something for the person, doing something for a cause the person would support, making a present, buying a gift, spending time with the person and so on.)

■ Do different people appreciate different ways of saying thank you? What would be a nice way to say thank you to an elderly person?

■ When do children need to thank others?

Monday

Dear Class

We would like to say thank you to the old man who gave us the magic beans. How can we say thank you?

Any ideas would be much appreciated.

Jack

and his mum

The Seven Little Kids

6

Some prompt questions/points to think about

These questions/prompts may be raised before writing the letters or afterwards in a discussion of the views expressed in the children's letters. Some may make good headings/questions on a display of the children's letters.

- How do you get rid of nightmares?
- Does having nightmares make you a babyish, weak or stupid person?
- Who can/do you talk to when you are upset or worried about something?
- Are there things that children may not like to talk about? Is this a good thing?

- What can you do when other people laugh at you?
- Are there some things you shouldn't discuss with your friends? With your family?

Goats Lane
Kiddie Town

Tuesday

Dear Class

Since the Wolf broke into our house,
I have been getting nightmares.
I can't discuss this with my brothers
and sisters – they would just laugh.
What can I do to stop the nightmares?
Please help.

Love
The Second Littlest Kid

Little Red Riding Hood

7

Some prompt questions/points to think about

These questions/prompts may be raised before writing the letters or afterwards in a discussion of the views expressed in the children's letters. Some may make good headings/questions on a display of the children's letters.

- Have you ever had to wear something that you didn't like?
- Why do children get teased for wearing something different?
- Does teasing matter or is Red Riding Hood just being oversensitive?
- What does teasing show about the 'teaser'?

- How can Red Riding Hood stop people teasing her (without buying new clothes)?
- Why does Mum make Red Riding Hood wear this? What is Mum's point of view?
- Is it a good use of money to buy expensive clothes for school?

---

11 Woodside
Near Wolf-Town

Wednesday

Dear Class

I am getting teased because Mum makes me wear this red riding hood to school. She won't buy me something more fashionable because she says it's warm and she's not made of money. What can I do?

Yours truly

Red Riding Hood

Snow White & the Seven Dwarves

8

Some prompt questions/points to think about

These questions/prompts may be raised before writing the letters or afterwards in a discussion of the views expressed in the children's letters. Some may make good headings/questions on a display of the children's letters.

- How might these items harm or hurt others?
- Who might be harmed or hurt by these items?
- How can accidents often be prevented?
- What do we need to think about if we are to find a way to keep them safely? For example, where and how the items are used, who will use them, who might misuse them?

- Where would the safest place be for each of these items?

Little Cottage
Smallville

Monday

Dear Class

I am keeping the Seven Dwarves' house tidy and clean. I need to put things, including all the cleaning products, in a safe place. Please write and suggest where I can put the:

- medicine
- bleach for the toilet
- bath cleaning gel
- razors (for shaving)
- kitchen knives.

Thank you

Snow White
— x —

The Elves & the Shoemaker

9

Some prompt questions/points to think about

These questions/prompts may be raised before writing the letters or afterwards in a discussion of the views expressed in the children's letters. Some may make good headings/questions on a display of the children's letters.

- How important is it to tidy up?
- Is it acceptable for Stitch to leave the tidying up to others if they do it for him (no matter how reluctantly)?
- What can Time do to let Stitch know how strongly he feels about this?

- What can Time do to make Stitch tidy up? Are there some things Time shouldn't do (even if they work)? Why? Are there some things he could try first/second/third?
- What rights and responsibilities does Stitch have? What about Time?

GOLDEN TOES SHOP

SHOE TOWN

Friday

Dear Class

Stitch has not been tidying up after we have been sewing all night. He says he has a very good reason. I don't think any excuse is good enough. I am so fed up that I don't want to play or work with Stitch any more.

Can you help?

Time (the smallest elf)

The Elves & the Shoemaker

10

Some prompt questions/points to think about

These questions/prompts may be raised before writing the letters or afterwards in a discussion of the views expressed in the children's letters. Some may make good headings/questions on a display of the children's letters.

- Who do the Elves need to talk to about this?
- Are holidays really necessary?
- How/when could making a plan help?
- How can a plan be recorded?

- Should the Elves tell the Shoemaker that his demands are too great?
- What are the Elves' rights and responsibilities?

GOLDEN TOES SHOP

SHOE TOWN

Tuesday

Dear Class

We are really exhausted and need a holiday, but the Shoemaker has had an order from the palace for 100 pairs of shoes. Some of them must be ready for the ball next month; others are for the summer garden party later on. Stitch, my brother elf, says we can fit in our work and a holiday. We just have to make a plan. Please help us to organise our work.

Thanks

Stitch

and Time (the Elves)

Snow White & the Seven Dwarves

11

Some prompt questions/points to think about

These questions/prompts may be raised before writing the letters or afterwards in a discussion of the views expressed in the children's letters. Some may make good headings/questions on a display of the children's letters.

■ How are the Dwarves feeling? (For example, lonely, bored, guilty, resentful, tired and so on.)
■ Can a person change how they feel? How?
■ Can recognising feelings/talking about feelings help a person overcome them?
■ Should the Dwarves tell Snow White how they feel? Should/could they tell anyone else?

■ Is it Snow White's fault that the Dwarves are feeling bad? Should she be asked to change her activities?
■ What should the Dwarves do to overcome their feelings?

Little Cottage
Smallville

Wednesday

Dear Class

Our house is very quiet and we are missing Snow White every day. She says she misses us too. But she is living with the Prince and is very busy having a lovely time. We are just moping around thinking about how nice things used to be. How can we make ourselves feel better about the situation?

Please help.

Doc
Dopey
Happy
Sneezey
Sleepy
Grumpy
Bashful

The Seven Dwarves

The Three Billy Goats Gruff

12

Some prompt questions/points to think about

These questions/prompts may be raised before writing the letters or afterwards in a discussion of the views expressed in the children's letters. Some may make good headings/questions on a display of the children's letters.

- Are friends necessary for everyone (even Trolls)?
- How do people make friends?
- Should the Troll look for lots of friends, or just a few (one?) good friend?

- What does the Troll need to change to become popular with others? (What he does? How he sees others? How he sees himself? What he wants from life?)
- How can others help the Troll change/make friends?

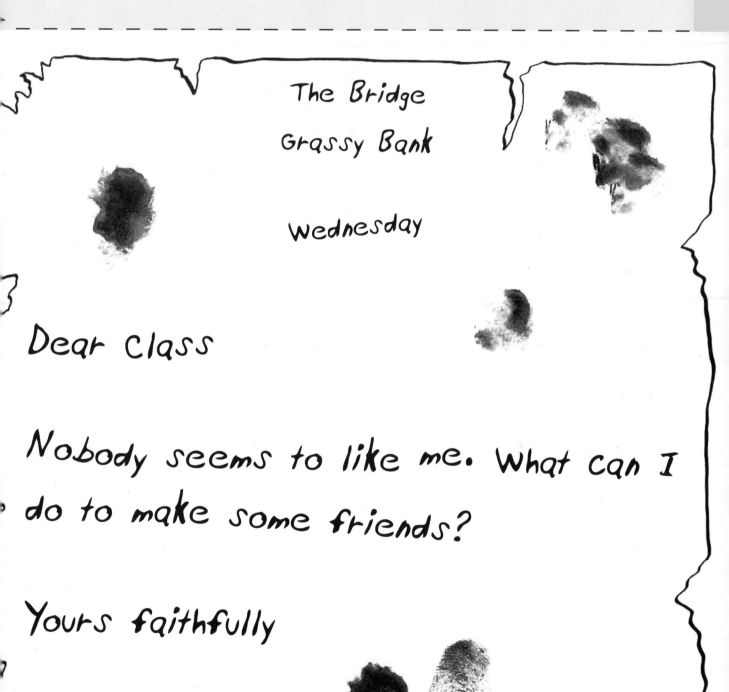

The Bridge

Grassy Bank

Wednesday

Dear class

Nobody seems to like me. What can I do to make some friends?

Yours faithfully

The Troll

Cinderella

13

Some prompt questions/points to think about

These questions/prompts may be raised before writing the letters or afterwards in a discussion of the views expressed in the children's letters. Some may make good headings/questions on a display of the children's letters.

- Can people who have done bad things change?
Must bad people always be bad?
- Should Cinderella forgive her Ugly Sisters, or not?
- How do you assess the value of a promise?

Saturday

Dear Class

I am now happily married and living with my prince. Yesterday, my Ugly Sisters wrote to ask if they could come and live with us at the palace. They promise that they will change their ways. Should I let them come? What do you think?

Yours faithfully

Cinderella

Goldilocks & the Three Bears

14

Some prompt questions/points to think about

These questions/prompts may be raised before writing the letters or afterwards in a discussion of the views expressed in the children's letters. Some may make good headings/questions on a display of the children's letters.

- How can you show someone you are sorry?
- Is stopping speaking to someone ever justified? Is it a good way to sort something out?
- How might Baby Bear see/feel about this? How might Goldilocks see/feel?
- Do accidents ever 'just happen'?

52 Wood Lane
Darksville

Friday

Dear Class

Baby Bear doesn't talk to me since I accidentally broke some of his stuff. How can I make him be friends?

Yours truly

Goldilocks

Little Red Riding Hood

Some prompt questions/points to think about

These questions/prompts may be raised before writing the letters or afterwards in a discussion of the views expressed in the children's letters. Some may make good headings/questions on a display of the children's letters.

■ Is it necessary/important to say thank you, even if you will see the person again? Why?

■ What are the different ways of saying thank you? (For example, sending a letter/card, doing something for the person, doing something for a cause the person would support, making a present, buying a gift, spending time with the person and so on.)

■ Do different people appreciate different things? What sort of person is the Woodcutter and what would be a nice way to say thank you to him?

■ Are there other jobs that old people such as Gran need help with?

**Red Cottage
Wolf Wood**

Monday

Dear Class

The Woodcutter has been really kind and helpful to me recently. First, he saved me and my grandaughter (Red Riding Hood) from the Wolf. Since then, he has tidied my garden and done several odd jobs around the house - he has fixed my roof and put a new lock on the door. I would like to do something to say thank you to him, but what can I do? Any ideas gratefully appreciated.

**Yours truly
Red Riding Hood's gran XXX**

Jack & the Beanstalk

16

Some prompt questions/points to think about

These questions/prompts may be raised before writing the letters or afterwards in a discussion of the views expressed in the children's letters. Some may make good headings/questions on a display of the children's letters.

- Whose job is it to tidy the bedroom?
- How could you explain Jack's viewpoint? His mother's viewpoint?
- Why is it important to tidy a bedroom? Does it matter if it is a mess?

- How could Jack/his mother persuade each other? Are there any persuasion methods that would probably work but should not be used? Why?
- Should children be rewarded for doing jobs around the house, or should they just help?
- Why does Jack want money? Is it more important than goodwill/his mother's respect?

Cosy House
Stalk Town

Tuesday

Dear Class

Now that we are rich, I think that Mum should pay me for tidying my bedroom. However, she doesn't agree. She says it's my room and my mess and that I should not expect a reward for clearing it up.

Who do you think is right?

Love Jack.

Goldilocks & the Three Bears

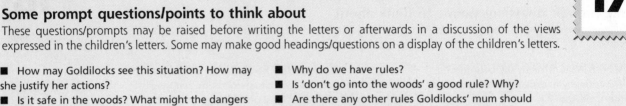

17

Some prompt questions/points to think about

These questions/prompts may be raised before writing the letters or afterwards in a discussion of the views expressed in the children's letters. Some may make good headings/questions on a display of the children's letters.

- How may Goldilocks see this situation? How may she justify her actions?
- Is it safe in the woods? What might the dangers be?
- What should Goldilocks' mum do to make her listen?

- Why do we have rules?
- Is 'don't go into the woods' a good rule? Why?
- Are there any other rules Goldilocks' mum should make? How can she express the rules in a positive way?

52 Wood Lane
Darksville

Thursday

Dear Class

My daughter Goldilocks keeps running off into the woods. She won't listen to a word I say. What can I do to make her listen and do as she is told?

Yours faithfully

Goldilocks' mum

Hansel & Gretel

18

Some prompt questions/points to think about

These questions/prompts may be raised before writing the letters or afterwards in a discussion of the views expressed in the children's letters. Some may make good headings/questions on a display of the children's letters.

■ What does it feel like to have no one to play with?

■ What can Gretel do about this? Who can she talk to?

■ Is there a difference between being lonely and being alone?

■ How do you make friends?

■ How might Hansel feel about this situation?

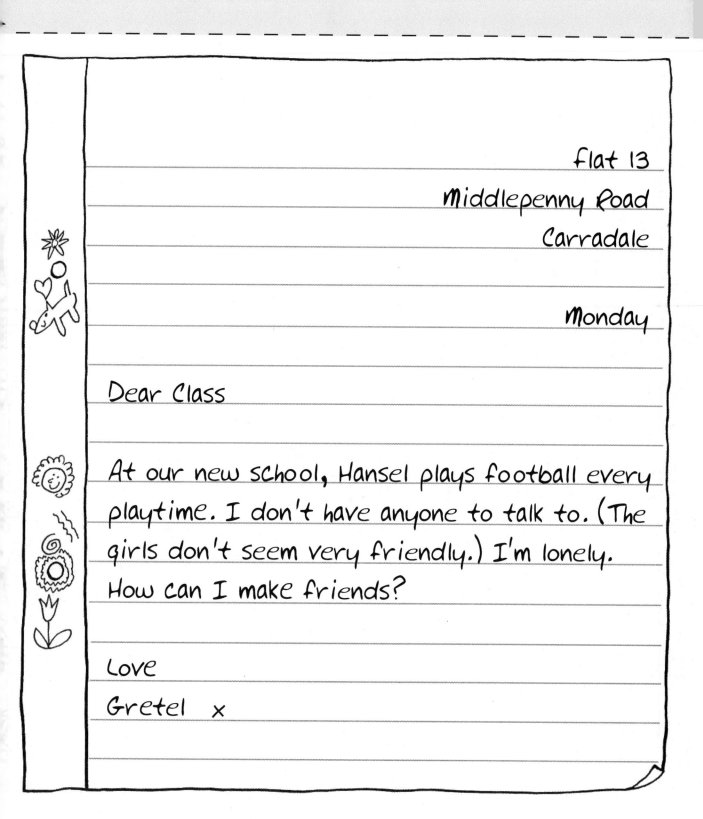

flat 13

Middlepenny Road

Carradale

Monday

Dear Class

At our new school, Hansel plays football every playtime. I don't have anyone to talk to. (The girls don't seem very friendly.) I'm lonely. How can I make friends?

Love

Gretel x

Hansel & Gretel

19

Some prompt questions/points to think about

These questions/prompts may be raised before writing the letters or afterwards in a discussion of the views expressed in the children's letters. Some may make good headings/questions on a display of the children's letters.

■ What are the main dangers Hansel and Gretel may meet?

■ What are the three most important things to remember to keep yourself safe in a town/city?

■ What is important to know about keeping safe at home?

flat 13

Middlepenny Road

Carradale

Tuesday

Dear Class

We have moved away from our house in the woods and are living in the city. It seems a dangerous place. There are lots of people and the roads are very busy. How can we keep ourselves safe when we come home after school?

Love

Hansel

and Gretel   x

Jack & the Beanstalk

Some prompt questions/points to think about

These questions/prompts may be raised before writing the letters or afterwards in a discussion of the views expressed in the children's letters. Some may make good headings/questions on a display of the children's letters.

- ■ Who might this money help in the world?
- ■ What is the difference between needs and wants?
- ■ How much of the money should they spend on themselves and how much on others?

Cosy House
Stalk Town

Dear Class

What do you think we should do with the money from the golden eggs? We'd like to spend some on ourselves and we'd also like to use some to do good in the world. Have you any suggestions?

Yours faithfully

Jack

and his mum

Hansel & Gretel

21

Some prompt questions/points to think about

These questions/prompts may be raised before writing the letters or afterwards in a discussion of the views expressed in the children's letters. Some may make good headings/questions on a display of the children's letters.

- Is Hansel being a bully, or is he just trying to help?
- How can Gretel help Hansel understand how she feels?
- Is there anyone that Gretel should talk to about her problems?

- Are there times when older children should tell younger ones what to do? Are there times when they shouldn't?

Flat 13

Middlepenny Road

Carradale

Dear Class

My brother Hansel is always bossing me about. He says he is older than me so I must do what he says. I don't see why I should. Dad just tells us to stop arguing. What can I do?

Love

Gretel xx

The Elves & the Shoemaker

Some prompt questions/points to think about

These questions/prompts may be raised before writing the letters or afterwards in a discussion of the views expressed in the children's letters. Some may make good headings/questions on a display of the children's letters.

- Is it necessary/important to say thank you?
- What are the different ways of saying thank you? (For example, sending a letter/card, doing something for the person, doing something for a cause the person would support, making a present, buying a gift, spending time with the person and so on.)

- What would be a nice way to say thank you to the Elves?
- When do children need to thank others?

Saturday

Golden Toes Shop
Shoe Town

Dear Class

The Elves made lots of shoes for a ball at the palace. The King would like to reward them for all their work. What can he do? (I have already given them clothes.) Any suggestions gratefully recieved.

Yours

The Shoemaker

The Three Billy Goats Gruff

Some prompt questions/points to think about

These questions/prompts may be raised before writing the letters or afterwards in a discussion of the views expressed in the children's letters. Some may make good headings/questions on a display of the children's letters.

- Do you think the Troll has really changed? Can people who have done bad things change or will they always be bad?
- How can you tell that someone is really sorry? How can people show they are sorry?

- Should the Billy Goats Gruff forgive? Are there some things that can never be forgiven?
- What could help the Billy Goats Gruff trust the Troll?
- Can you see this from the Troll's viewpoint?

**GOATY COTTAGE
HILLSIDE**

Monday

Dear Class

The Troll has moved back into his cave under the bridge. He says that he has learnt his lesson, and we can go back and forth as often as we like. Our problem is this: can we trust the Troll?

Any advice would be appreciated.

Yours

The Three Billy Goats Gruff

Little Red Riding Hood

24

Some prompt questions/points to think about

These questions/prompts may be raised before writing the letters or afterwards in a discussion of the views expressed in the children's letters. Some may make good headings/questions on a display of the children's letters.

- Can you see this problem from Gran's viewpoint? Mum's viewpoint?
- Is there another way to solve this problem?
- What rights and responsibilities does Red Riding Hood have?

---

11 Woodside
Near Wolf-Town

Tuesday

Dear Class

Now the woods are safe I can take a shortcut to Gran's house. The trouble is, now she expects me to go there every day. I want to stay home and play with my friends, but Mum makes me go. She says Gran is lonely and likes my company. It's not fair. I don't see why I have to go all the time. What do you think?

Yours sincerely

Red Riding Hood

Hansel & Gretel

25

Some prompt questions/points to think about

These questions/prompts may be raised before writing the letters or afterwards in a discussion of the views expressed in the children's letters. Some may make good headings/questions on a display of the children's letters.

■ Should Hansel stand up for Gretel? Would it matter if he did/didn't?
■ What can Gretel do? What advice can you give to someone who is being bullied?
■ How do you stop people from teasing you?

■ Should Hansel (or Gretel) talk to anyone about this? Who?
■ Can you see this from the bully's perspective?
■ How do you make friends?
■ What rights does Gretel have? Can younger children stop older children picking on them?

Flat 13
Middlepenny Road
Carradale

Friday

Dear Class

I am getting along quite well with the people at our new school. However, Gretel is shy and not so confident. One of the older girls has taken a dislike to her. She is going around saying, "If you are friends with Gretel, you can't come to my party." She is also encouraging other people to tease her. Gretel hasn't got any friends and I know it's making her very miserable. If I stand up for Gretel, they will just start picking on me as well. Please tell me what to do.

Hansel

Goldilocks & the Three Bears

Some prompt questions/points to think about

These questions/prompts may be raised before writing the letters or afterwards in a discussion of the views expressed in the children's letters. Some may make good headings/questions on a display of the children's letters.

■ Is Baby Bear right to be worried? How do you judge when worries are well founded/unfounded?
■ Baby Bear is scared, but does this make Goldilocks a bully?
■ Should Baby Bear speak to Goldilocks? What might be the consequences of being aggressive to

her? Of trying to make friends with her? Of refusing to speak to her?
■ Can Baby Bear and Goldilocks change their views of each other?
■ How do you think Goldilocks sees this situation?

Bear Cottage
Wood Lane
Darksville

Dear Class

Last year, when I was four years old, a horrible thing happened. This girl Goldilocks broke into my house. She ate my porridge, broke my chair and slept on my bed. Ma and Pa frightened her away.

Now I am five years old and have just started a new school. The teacher is kind and nice, but guess who is sitting at my table? Goldilocks! She hasn't said anything yet, but I am worried. What should I do?

Yours sincerely

Baby Bear

The Elves & the Shoemaker

Some prompt questions/points to think about

These questions/prompts may be raised before writing the letters or afterwards in a discussion of the views expressed in the children's letters. Some may make good headings/questions on a display of the children's letters.

■ Do you know someone that the Elves might be able to help?

■ Can you think of people in the wider community/world who might need help?

■ What are the different types of help people may require – material needs, emotional/social needs (For example, companionship, confidence?)

■ What is the difference between needs and wants?

■ How could the Elves weigh the different claims and decide whom to help? (What criteria could they use?)

■ Do all the things children suggest actually need magic, or are some within our own/other people's control? What could we do to help others?

GOLDEN TOES SHOP

SHOE TOWN

Friday

Dear Class

The Shoemaker has now got lots of food and money and we feel that we should go and help someone else. Do you know anyone who could do with some help? We have made shoes, but can also turn our hands to most tasks.

Please write with your suggestions. We can only help one person, so remember to explain why you think this person deserves our help.

Many thanks

Stitch and Time

Goldilocks & the Three Bears

28

Some prompt questions/points to think about

These questions/prompts may be raised before writing the letters or afterwards in a discussion of the views expressed in the children's letters. Some may make good headings/questions on a display of the children's letters.

- Why may Baby Bear not want such a meeting?
- Why do you think Goldilocks has invited Baby Bear round for tea?
- Why does Ma Bear want Baby Bear to go?
- What are the advantages/disadvantages of such a meeting?
- How can Baby Bear help Ma to understand his feelings?

Bear Cottage
Wood Lane
Darksville

Dear Class

Goldilocks has asked me round to tea. Ma says I should go to be polite, but I really don't like her. What should I do?

Yours truly

Baby Bear

Cinderella

29

Some prompt questions/points to think about

These questions/prompts may be raised before writing the letters or afterwards in a discussion of the views expressed in the children's letters. Some may make good headings/questions on a display of the children's letters.

- In what sort of ways can anger show itself?
- Why do you think the Ugly Sister may get angry with Cinderella?
- How can people control their anger? What helps? How does it help?

- Is it important to control anger?
- Is it enough to say sorry?

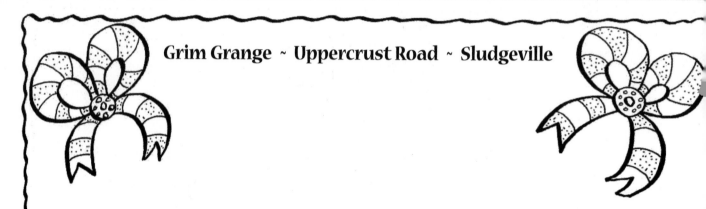

Grim Grange ~ Uppercrust Road ~ Sludgeville

Wednesday

Dear Class

I know I should be nicer to Cinderella,
but sometimes I just get so cross that
I can't control my temper. How can I
stop myself being so nasty to her?

Yours faithfully

An Ugly Sister (the taller one)

The Seven Little Kids

30

Some prompt questions/points to think about

These questions/prompts may be raised before writing the letters or afterwards in a discussion of the views expressed in the children's letters. Some may make good headings/questions on a display of the children's letters.

■ What things can you try when someone is doing something you don't like?

■ Can you see this from the littlest brother's viewpoint?

■ Are there things that would make the brothers feel better, but shouldn't be done? Why?

■ What would help the littlest brother realise that he has become too big for his boots?

■ Do people change?

Goats Lane

Kiddie Town

Wednesday

Dear Class

Our littlest brother hid in the clock case and saved us all from the Wolf. Now he keeps bossing us about and gets in a huff if we don't do what he says. He used to be nice, but now he has just too big an opinion of himself. How can we take him down a peg or two?

Yours faithfully

The Six Kid Brothers

Jack & the Beanstalk

Some prompt questions/points to think about

These questions/prompts may be raised before writing the letters or afterwards in a discussion of the views expressed in the children's letters. Some may make good headings/questions on a display of the children's letters.

- Do you think Jack or his mum is right? Why?
- What is the difference between needs and wants?
- What else could Jack do with his money?
- Is it a good thing to instantly get everything you want?

- Can money/toys buy you happiness?
- What can/can't money buy?
- Does Jack's mother have the right to tell him what to do? Does Jack have the right to refuse?

Tuesday

Dear Class

Jack and I have been arguing about money. In my opinion he is spending too much – the house is littered with toys and useless gadgets. He says it is his hen and he can do what he likes. I say that I am his mother and he should do what I tell him. What do you think?

Yours truly

Jack's mum

The Three Billy Goats Gruff

32

Some prompt questions/points to think about
These questions/prompts may be raised before writing the letters or afterwards in a discussion of the views expressed in the children's letters. Some may make good headings/questions on a display of the children's letters.

- Do you think the Billy Goats Gruff should go into the cave? Why/Why not?
- What are the rules about entering someone else's house?
- When can rules be broken? Should some rules never be broken?
- What rights does the Troll have? What rights do the Billy Goats have?

GOATY COTTAGE
HILLSIDE

Monday

Dear Class

We are fairly sure that the Troll has gone for good.
We are very curious about what is in his cave under the bridge.
It might be treasure. Do you think it would be all right to break
into his house and have a look?

Yours faithfully

The Three Billy Goats Gruff

The Seven Little Kids

Some prompt questions/points to think about

These questions/prompts may be raised before writing the letters or afterwards in a discussion of the views expressed in the children's letters. Some may make good headings/questions on a display of the children's letters.

■ What/who is right and wrong in this situation? Why?

■ How do the Littlest Kid's brothers feel? Does this justify/explain their actions?

■ Can you see this situation from the Baker's viewpoint? Does this justify/explain his actions? Why may he have let the Wolf use his flour? How might he feel about the Kids now?

■ What should the Littlest Kid do?

■ How can you resist pressure from your friends?

Goats Lane
Kiddie Town

~~Thurs~~ Thursday

Dear Class

My brothers and their friends keep doing horrid things to the Baker who let the Wolf put ~~flowe~~ flour and dough on his paws to deceive us. If I don't join in, I know that they won't play with me. I do want to be part of their crowd – most of the time they are good fun to be with – so should I just go along with what they say?

Yours truly

The Littlest Kid

Hansel & Gretel

34

Some prompt questions/points to think about

These questions/prompts may be raised before writing the letters or afterwards in a discussion of the views expressed in the children's letters. Some may make good headings/questions on a display of the children's letters.

- What advice would you give Hansel?
- Being scared implies that you can imagine things that haven't yet happened. Do some people have bigger imaginations than others?
- Is it wrong to admit/show you are scared?

- How can Hansel assess/minimise the risks involved?
- Who can Hansel talk to about his feelings?
- How can you resist pressure from your friends?

Flat 13
Middlepenny Road
Carradale

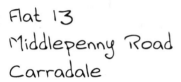

Tuesday

Dear Class

A while ago, my sister and I had a terrible experience in the woods. Since then, I've made sure I stay near shops and houses and have never gone into the woods, alone or with anyone else.

However, I have just found out that our new school trip involves camping in the woods. I have tried explaining how I feel to Gretel, but she just says that boys are supposed to be brave and there must be something wrong with me if I am frightened.

Please give me some advice.

Best regards
Hansel

The Three Little Pigs

35

Some prompt questions/points to think about

These questions/prompts may be raised before writing the letters or afterwards in a discussion of the views expressed in the children's letters. Some may make good headings/questions on a display of the children's letters.

- Can you see this from the brothers' viewpoints?
- What might be the consequences of asking the brothers to move out?
- How can suggestions be framed to minimise the brothers' hurt feelings?

- Are there things that each of the Pigs needs to learn from this situation?
- What are the rights/responsibilities of the Eldest Pig? His brothers?

**Brick House
Piggy Town**

Friday

Dear Class

My brothers moved in with me after the Wolf blew down their houses. Although I like my brothers, my house is small (it was only built for one pig), and I liked living on my own. My brothers show no signs of moving out into their own accommodation. How can I ask them to leave without hurting their feelings?

Yours sincerely

The Eldest Pig

Jack & the Beanstalk

36

Some prompt questions/points to think about

These questions/prompts may be raised before writing the letters or afterwards in a discussion of the views expressed in the children's letters. Some may make good headings/questions on a display of the children's letters.

■ How can you tell who is a true friend?
■ Does it matter if people only want to be friends with Jack now that he has money?
■ What influences people to become your friend? What influences you to befriend others?

Cosy House
Stalk Town

Dear Class

Since we got rich, lots of people want to be friends with me. They are all very nice, but they didn't notice me when I was poor. Does this matter?

Please give me some advice.

Love from Jack

Little Red Riding Hood

37

Some prompt questions/points to think about

These questions/prompts may be raised before writing the letters or afterwards in a discussion of the views expressed in the children's letters. Some may make good headings/questions on a display of the children's letters.

- What are Granny's rights and responsibilities?
- What are the advantages/disadvantages of living alone? Living with others?
- How do you think Granny feels about this situation?
- Is it right to force people to do things they don't want?
- What is the actual problem here? Are there other ways to solve this problem?

11 Woodside
Near Wolf-Town

Wednesday

Dear Class

I think Granny should come and live with us. She's obviously not safe on her own. Granny, however, says she likes her cottage and she won't move. Would it be right to force her to move in with us?

Yours faithfully

Red Riding Hood's mum

Cinderella

38

Some prompt questions/points to think about

These questions/prompts may be raised before writing the letters or afterwards in a discussion of the views expressed in the children's letters. Some may make good headings/questions on a display of the children's letters.

- Why does the Prince want to marry Cinderella?
- What do the Ugly Sisters need to change (inside and out) to make themselves more attractive?

- Is it right to try to change the Prince's mind? How would Cinderella feel?
- Are there some things that money can't buy?

Grim Grange ~ Uppercrust Road ~ Sludgeville

Friday

Dear Class

We have spent a fortune on clothes and beauty treatments, but the Prince insists on marrying Cinderella.
How can we convince him that he is making a terrible mistake and would be better off marrying one of us?

Yours

The Ugly Sisters

Snow White & the Seven Dwarves

39

Some prompt questions/points to think about

These questions/prompts may be raised before writing the letters or afterwards in a discussion of the views expressed in the children's letters. Some may make good headings/questions on a display of the children's letters.

■ How can punishment be used to: control a person/prevent them from reoffending; make a person stop and consider their actions/feel sorry for their actions; make someone who has been wronged feel better?

■ Should we always forgive and forget? Are there some things that should not be forgiven and forgotten?
■ Can bad people change, or will they always be bad?
■ Do the stepmother's actions matter since everything turned out well in the end?

The Royal Castle
Buckinghamton

Monday

Dear Class

I am now happily married to the Prince. Everything has turned out well except for one thing: the Prince says he wants to punish my stepmother for what she did to me. He wants revenge. I know she was bad, but I'm not so sure that she should be punished. What do you think?

I need your advice.

Love

Snow White
—x—

The Three Billy Goats Gruff

40

Some prompt questions/points to think about

These questions/prompts may be raised before writing the letters or afterwards in a discussion of the views expressed in the children's letters. Some may make good headings/questions on a display of the children's letters.

- Are friends necessary for everyone (even Trolls and Billy Goats)?
- How could you persuade the Troll and the Billy Goats to become friends?
- How can you help the Troll/Billy Goats Gruff understand each other's viewpoint?

- Was the Big Billy Goat Gruff right to hurt the Troll? Was the Troll right to not let anyone use his bridge?
- What are the rules about respecting property? Sharing things?

The Bridge
Grassy Bank

Monday

Dear Class

The Big Billy Goat Gruff really hurt me, just because I wouldn't let him cross my bridge. From my point of view, it's <u>MY</u> bridge and I don't see why I should let them use it. They've never been very nice to me.

What do you think?

The Troll

Little Red Riding Hood

41

Some prompt questions/points to think about

These questions/prompts may be raised before writing the letters or afterwards in a discussion of the views expressed in the children's letters. Some may make good headings/questions on a display of the children's letters.

- Who do you think has the more compelling reason, Red Riding Hood or her mum?
- What is the real problem here? Is there a different way to solve it?

- Is there a difference between being alone and being lonely?
- How could Red Riding Hood persuade her mum? Should she do this?

---

11 Woodside
Near Wolf-Town

Friday

Dear Class

I hate living in this house by the woods. I have no friends to play with and nothing to do. Mum says we can't move to the town because she wants to stay near Gran. What can I do?

Yours faithfully

Red Riding Hood

Jack & the Beanstalk

42

Some prompt questions/points to think about

These questions/prompts may be raised before writing the letters or afterwards in a discussion of the views expressed in the children's letters. Some may make good headings/questions on a display of the children's letters.

- Who might benefit most from this money?
- What is the difference between needs and wants?
- What rights and responsibilities do Jack and his mother have to themselves? To each other? To the wider world?

- What needs/wants may Jack and his mother think about in the future?
- Is it important to share things like money?

Cosy House
Stalk Town

Thursday

Dear Class

We are down to our last golden egg. (We spent all the others on toys, having a good time and on buying things for the house.) Jack says we should give this last egg to charity (there are still a lot of poor people about.) I think we should spend it on ourselves, since it is the last one. What would you do?

Best regards

Jack's mum

Little Red Riding Hood

43

Some prompt questions/points to think about

These questions/prompts may be raised before writing the letters or afterwards in a discussion of the views expressed in the children's letters. Some may make good headings/questions on a display of the children's letters.

■ Is this the only possible solution to the problem? How else could Granny be supported?

■ What would be the advantages/disadvantages of living together: for Granny? For Red Riding Hood and her mum?

■ How can Granny ensure her own safety?

■ What do you think Granny should do? Why?

Red Cottage
Wolf Wood

Dear Class

Since the Wolf broke into my house, Red Riding Hood's mum has been worried about me. She says I should go and live with them (they have a very nice spare room). I don't want to cause her any worry, but I like my little cottage and I like living on my own. What should I do?

Yours truly

Red Riding Hood's granny XXX

The Elves & the Shoemaker

44

Some prompt questions/points to think about

These questions/prompts may be raised before writing the letters or afterwards in a discussion of the views expressed in the children's letters. Some may make good headings/questions on a display of the children's letters.

- Is there such a thing as a good/bad secret? What is the difference between good and bad secrets?
- Is it ever right to tell lies?
- What are the rights and responsibilities of the Elves? The Shoemaker? The friends/family?

Thursday

Golden Toes Shop
Shoe Town

Dear Class

The Elves don't want anyone to know about them, and I promised I wouldn't tell. The trouble is, people keep asking me about how I make these wonderful shoes. Even my best friend and my family have been asking. Should I lie to them all, or should I tell the truth and betray my promise?

Please give me advice.

Yours worriedly

The Shoemaker

The Seven Little Kids

45

Some prompt questions/points to think about

These questions/prompts may be raised before writing the letters or afterwards in a discussion of the views expressed in the children's letters. Some may make good headings/questions on a display of the children's letters.

- How do you judge whether someone is nice?
- Is playing a trick bullying?
- Is fear ever a just cause of aggression?
- What rights do the Little Kids have? What responsibilities do they have?

Goats Lane

Kiddie Town

Wednesday

Dear Class

The old wolf lived quite near us. He was horrible and got his comeuppance when Mum rescued us from his belly and filled it with stones. Now, a new wolf has moved into the house. Should we make this wolf welcome, or start playing tricks on him to make him move away?

Yours faithfully

Seven Little Kids

The Three Little Pigs

46

Some prompt questions/points to think about

These questions/prompts may be raised before writing the letters or afterwards in a discussion of the views expressed in the children's letters. Some may make good headings/questions on a display of the children's letters.

- How can the Little Pigs know that the Wolf has really changed?
- Can bad people change?
- How can the Little Pigs ensure their future safety?

- What are the advantages/disadvantages of being friends with the Wolf?
- Is it wrong to not want to be friends with someone?
- Is 'not speaking' ever a good way to settle a dispute?

10 Primrose Hill
Piggy Town

Monday

Dear Class

When we first moved in, the Wolf was nasty to us. That was years ago. Since then, he keeps saying he wants to be friends and has tried to be nice a few times. The two of us say we don't like him, but now our oldest brother thinks we should make a new start. He says that we're being as nasty as him by continuing the feud. What do you think?

We look forward to hearing your advice.

The Two Little Pigs

Jack & the Beanstalk

47

Some prompt questions/points to think about

These questions/prompts may be raised before writing the letters or afterwards in a discussion of the views expressed in the children's letters. Some may make good headings/questions on a display of the children's letters.

- What are Jack's current/future needs?
- What rights and responsibilities does Jack have?
- What is the difference between needs and wants?
- Do you think it is a good idea to save or spend? Why?

Cosy House
Stalk Town

Friday

Dear Class

Mum and I can't agree on what to do about the golden eggs. Mum says that the hen might not keep laying golden eggs for ever and we should save them. I say we've always been poor and we should enjoy spending the money. Who do you think is right?

Yours truly

Jack.

Snow White & the Seven Dwarves

48

Some prompt questions/points to think about

These questions/prompts may be raised before writing the letters or afterwards in a discussion of the views expressed in the children's letters. Some may make good headings/questions on a display of the children's letters.

- Does Snow White have the right to ask Grumpy to wash/make his bed?
- What are the advantages of being clean/tidy?
- Can you see this from Grumpy's viewpoint?
- What is the real problem here? How can they negotiate a solution?
- What responsibilities does Grumpy have to himself? To others?

Little Cottage
Smallville

Dear Class

Grumpy doesn't seem to like Snow White. He won't wash himself or make his bed like she asks him to. He says it is his right to be dirty if he wants to be. Who do you think is right, Grumpy or Snow White?

Yours sincerely

Doc

The Three Little Pigs

49

Some prompt questions/points to think about

These questions/prompts may be raised before writing the letters or afterwards in a discussion of the views expressed in the children's letters. Some may make good headings/questions on a display of the children's letters.

- Is it all right for the Wolf to eat the Pigs?
- What rights and responsibilities do the Pigs have?
- What rights and responsibilities does the Wolf have?

- What is the problem here? What else could the Wolf eat and still be healthy?

5 Windy Block
Stoney Hill

Thursday

Dear Class

Everyone thinks badly of me because I tried to eat the Three Little Pigs. But I say, look at me closely: long black snout, thick hair – I'm a wolf, for goodness sake! Pigs are what wolves are supposed to eat! I don't think I did anything wrong. Do you?

Yours faithfully

Wolfie

The Three Billy Goats Gruff

50

Some prompt questions/points to think about

These questions/prompts may be raised before writing the letters or afterwards in a discussion of the views expressed in the children's letters. Some may make good headings/questions on a display of the children's letters.

■ Were the Middle and Big Billy Goats right or wrong? Why?

■ What can people do if they have nightmares?

■ Does the end justify the means? Should the Littlest Billy Goat forgive and forget?

■ Is trust important? How do you recover the trust of others?

■ How can the Billy Goats resolve their differences? Are some ways more effective than others?

GOATY COTTAGE
HILLSIDE

Tuesday

Dear Class

The Littlest Billy Goat Gruff keeps saying that he doesn't think it was right that we let him walk over the bridge and face the Troll alone. He says it has given him nightmares and he doesn't think he can rely on us in a crisis.

We don't see what the problem is — after all, it all worked out well in the end. We think he should stop going on about it.

What do you think?

Regards

Middle and Big Billy Goat Gruff

TALES INDEX

Tale	Letters
Goldilocks & the Three Bears	1, 14, 17, 26, 28
The Three Little Pigs	2, 35, 46, 49
Cinderella	3, 13, 29, 38
Snow White & the Seven Dwarves	4, 8, 11, 39, 48
Jack & the Beanstalk	5, 16, 20, 31, 36, 42, 47
The Seven Little Kids	6, 30, 33, 45
Little Red Riding Hood	7, 15, 24, 37, 41, 43
The Elves & the Shoemaker	9, 10, 22, 27, 44
The Three Billy Goats Gruff	12, 23, 32, 40, 50
Hansel & Gretel	18, 19, 21, 25, 34